ELECTRIC SHADOW

Born in Norfolk in 1971, **Heidi Williamson** has lived in central Scotland, Brussels and Salisbury. She now lives in Wymondham, Norfolk. She is an Advisory Fellow for the Royal Literary Fund, and was Royal Literary Fund Fellow at the University of East Anglia from 2018 to 2020. From 2011 to 2014, she was writer-in-residence at the John Jarrold Printing Museum in Norwich and in 2008-09 was poet-in-residence at the London Science Museum's Dana Centre. In 2008 she received an Arts Council award to complete her first collection, *Electric Shadow* (Bloodaxe Books, 2011), a Poetry Book Society Recommendation, which was shortlisted for the Seamus Heaney Centre for Poetry Prize. *The Print Museum* (Bloodaxe Books, 2016) won the Poetry Category and the Book by the Cover award in the 2016 East Anglian Book Awards. Her third collection, *Return by Minor Road*, was published by Bloodaxe Books in 2020.

Her work has been used to inspire poetry and science discussions in schools and adult creative writing groups, and has featured in NHS waiting rooms, cafés, and at festivals. Poems have been translated into Polish, Turkish, Romanian and German. She works with poets worldwide by Skype as a poetry surgeon for The Poetry Society, teaches for The Poetry School, and mentors poets through The Writing Coach, National Centre for Writing and The Poetry School. For more information, see her website www.heidiwilliamsonpoet.com

HEIDI WILLIAMSON

Electric Shadow

BLOODAXE BOOKS

ISBN: 978 1 85224 902 1

First published 2011 by
Bloodaxe Books Ltd,
Eastburn,
South Park,
Hexham,
Northumberland NE46 1BS.

www.bloodaxebooks.com
For further information about Bloodaxe titles
please visit our website and join our mailing list
or write to the above address for a catalogue.

Supported using public funding by
**ARTS COUNCIL
ENGLAND**

Cover design: Neil Astley & Pamela Robertson-Pearce.

Digital reprint of the 2011 Bloodaxe Books edition.

For G

ACKNOWLEDGEMENTS

Acknowledgements are due to the editors of the following publications and websites where some of these poems first appeared: www.danacentre.org.uk; guardian.co.uk, *Gift*, ed. Tom Corbett & Helen Ivory (Gatehouse Press); *Horizon Review*; *Ink, Sweat and Tears*; *Iota*; *Mslexia*; *Poetry News*; *Obsessed by Pipework*; *Orbis*; *Other Poetry*; *Penumbra*; *The Rialto*; *Smoke*; *South*; *Voicing Visions* exhibition catalogue.

'Slide rule' won the Poetry Can Poetry Competition 2009. 'Emily Cohen knits summer' was a runner up in the Mslexia Poetry Competition 2008. 'The slip' was a runner up in the Mslexia Poetry Competition 2007. 'France, 1941' was shortlisted for The Poetry Society Hamish Canham Prize 2008; it was also nominated for the Forward Prize for Best Single Poem, as was 'Arachne'.

I am grateful to Arts Council England for a writer's grant to work on this collection, and to the London Science Museum's Dana Centre for my residency there in 2008 and 2009.

I would like to thank Bex Barrow, Clare Jarrett, Nina Robertson, Bridget Beauchamp, Sally Paramour, Archie Clifford, Helen Ivory, Sarah Law, Stephen Payne, Esther Morgan and Tamar Yoseloff for all their advice and encouragement. Thanks also to all at Norwich Café Writers.

CONTENTS

Slide rule

The universe is running away with itself
like a child on a red bike on Christmas Day.

Somewhere the wrapping is still being opened.
The present gives itself again and again.

And the child hurtles at perfect speed
across town towards nothing.

Her parents are already
looking at the clock, saying

how late it is getting, how the darkness
comes so much sooner.

It is only a matter of time,
they are saying,

before she will land,
awkwardly, in an original position,

sucking in broken concrete
and teeth.

Meanwhile,
the child on a red bike

is running away with herself
like the universe on Christmas Day.

East looking East

She is in the East, looking East,
as the world turns against
the principles of stability.

Knowing that a star's light
sweeps the world's surface
towards evening doesn't halt

the arc of the sun as she sees it.
It goes against instinct to feel
she is wheeling in circles in space.

She knows the Earth tilts East,
23° from its vertical axis – as if
all uncertainty can be cleared

by knowing the angle of light
on her palm. She knows the reason
her days lengthen and shorten,

why her palms crease with shadows,
that space is only one mile up,
closer than the next town,

that the sun is nuclear.
Evening brings more chances
to recognise where she stands –

as the waters darken
and a clear sky leaves her
cold with stars.

Cosmonaut

To know I am in quarantine
and not to be touched,
that the world cannot
taint me – it pains me.

On the other side of the glass
my family waits. I wanted only
to see the world distant, a simple
light in the sky – to see the earth rise.

I had not considered it would feel
like an amputation. Meanings rise
and stream from me like sunsets. Silence
deepens our goodbye. I cannot discern

any last trace of your voice
with all the worlds there are between us.

If Then Else

If
your lover asks you to bite his tongue, Then
do it
Else you are alone and bloodless

If
you cannot find yourself, Then
find another
Else you are alive and loveless

If
you breathe numbness, Then
rejoice quietly
Else you are woken

If
you age, Then
live
Else you age lifelessly

If
you die, Then
think
Else you die thoughtlessly

If
you wish to eat apples and oranges, Then
choose
Else no distinctions can be made

If Then Else: A logic statement in high-level programming that defines the data to be compared and the actions to be taken as a result. There can only be one of two outcomes. There is no scope for ambiguity.

France, 1941

My mouth will not open for the soldier
seated in my father's chair. He knows now

and inclines his head in polite salute,
indifferent as a cat. I will my bones

not to react, reflect – as the impulse travels
through my senses I quash it. I am skilled

in the texture of silence. But at night
he eases Chopin into the air, lets

the quiet in the music carry. He taps
his pipe and cocks his head to listen.

In the stillness of my room I hold
my breath. All the meaning I will not give

forms in the air
like lengthened notes, a gift.

'A' Level text

Le Blé en Herbe ('The Awakening') by Colette

It seems I read all summer,
tanned feet stretched,
levellers on hot ruffs of rock.
I sought a coast I'd never met,
greeted the far start of the sea:
the sun fused me to its scent.
My toes quarried scorched sand,
rough grass punctured my soles,
sea-snails stirred in whorled casings.
I glimpsed shells like young bones.
Gulls shouted common phrases.
Words streamed the Breton sky.
The air about me foreign,
taut, I collected shells of meaning
I turn again against my tongue.

Woodcutter

In a school room, the woodcutter
had come for the children.

Every wolf that he could muster,
the bears, the dwarves, the witches

herded them into the darkened forest.
Once there, they tried to be small

as birds, quieter, one feather
pressed to their beaks.

They practised soaring
against the sound of metal.

The adults began to sing softly,
cooed like infants to still the flapping.

The woodcutter stalked the oaks
and called to them with his shiny voice.

The children lay their heads
beneath their wings and waited.

The slip

Six months after the first skeleton
appeared we are used to the slip

between the plate and the mouth,
my daughter's bargains against food.

Her eyes weigh the fat content used
or imposed in water, movement, air.

She is climbing the mast of a ship
none of us can steer.

It is this one small thing she wants:
not to change, or only to change

on her own terms, badly.
I spoon each mouthful myself,

attempt to navigate her closed lips,
try not to notice the looseness

of my grip, the thinness of the skin
on my own wrist.

Hodgkin's hands

They were not the tools you wanted:
bent against minute designs,
intent on their own future.
With molecules splayed
against film, you mapped
what makes us,
what made you.

All the while
you must have studied them,
inconstant equipment
you could not update,
showing you daily
what you knew best:
the body has its own plans.

You could only control
(with the patience scientists know
or practise) their variations,
make adjustments,
work with, not against,
their root-like searching
for stability in shifting cells.

X-ray crystallographer Dorothy Hodgkin won
the Nobel Prize in Chemistry despite suffering
from severely arthritic hands from the age of 24.

Williamson County gloves

My lover sends me cowboy gloves
bought in a county named for me.
The leather is unbroken, musky
as stallion's flanks. I trace
the smooth edge of each finger,
lay them by me at night: become
a rolling, low, black land, guarded
out west by limestone hills, swathed
in prairie grasses – somewhere
grain and cotton prosper, delicate
but fulsome, blowsy in Atlantic breezes.
My dreams range with a candour I lack
when awake. I lick the leather,
watch the wet darkness linger.

Emily Cohen knits summer

A small suburban garden with absent
birds. The *clack-clack* is only
Emily's needles clashing.

She knits for her younger sister's bump.
Her wool is the pale yellow
of indeterminate sex.

The small cardigan's arms flex,
ageing her as they grow.
She concentrates on the clouds.

She's aware of the gap
where summer should be.
This year only rain has bloomed.

Her work done, she holds it up
to the grim August day –
such a small thing, its beginnings

untraceable now.
She packs up her things,
her hands shaking.

The garden is silent – her rage
at its silence surprising.
Such a small thing.

Cordwainers

They understand about loss –
the way leather sighs

as it shifts round an awl,
how boar bristles reach

tight into curves
to keep the thread from chafing,

that helling sticks
and bones are vital

for softness to be forced in,
that each burnished stitch is

easy to work in,
hellish to work out,

that making, though coveted,
is harsh on the heart.

Making shoes from skin

In the bottom of the wardrobe like dead bodies
Lana's shoes accrue. Each day she digs
for fresh treasure and slips into skins
as easily as sleeping. She walks on bone.

Having grown up at the heels of men
she knows every step is a line
to be crossed, every flaw is a chance
to be beaten out. Old things get thrown.

Lana piles her victories high. Man-made
whims of sinew and leather gather
before her. Every day is an open door
to all those tongues hanging out.

Brodsky at the milling machine

'Who recognises you as a poet?
Who enrolled you in the ranks of poets?'
                    Joseph Brodsky trial for parasitism, 1963

I think of Brodsky at the milling machine,
as he works metal against metal,
grinds out precise shapes:

the stress of carving every form,
each breath forced out by a blow,
as all materials submit at length.

Where is his mind as his body acts
at its station: lifts and places,
lowers, guides and oversees?

Does he worry each piece is too tidy
for the mess of bone, sinew and blood?
Or does he study the robust shine

of the finished piece, satisfied
it will find its own way to break
any tender being?

James Dean escorts his mother's coffin

The rocking of the train as it crosses the country
lulls you as the land you know peels away
into the past. You are nine. Your small face
echoes on the polished surface of her coffin.
Your father has sent you away.

Each stop you check your tender cargo
is not yet lost. You caress the smooth wood,
warm from the heat of strangers' breathing.
The world speeds past, begins to blur to nothing.
You will always remember these moments.

She taught you the wishing game. You cradle
the snipped lock of her hair and play it alone.
You pretend to keep faith in the possible
but cannot accept this new cargo's silence.
Something inside you is peeling away.

You wonder how fine handles carry such weight.
Placing your hands on the cold brass you grasp
the frailty of the thin plane between you.
Somewhere within you a small cargo shifts.
Some things take a lifetime to travel past.

The grand dance

There is a partner I cannot see
bewildering my sense of how to move.

I want to let go, step away. But always pressure
pushes me on. There is no stillness.

I have to trip forwards. And whenever I turn
my head, his hand is always there

and not there, against my cheek.
His presence silts the air.

There are no steps here. There is no learning.
Only forwards and back, forwards and back,

towards and away –
a grand dance I can never move on from.

At the hands-on science centre

After the voice distorter and the tubed tornado,
two slivers of parallel mirrors, thin and silent,
like a gate. We stand laughing between them
on the white line, as indicated, and salute
our many selves. A slide to the right leaves
a curved staircase of ghosts rising behind us.
We spool endlessly away, the real us just
a frame in a film running before and after.
Our fronts and backs alternate, never
meet, like the two sides of glass, apart
but linked by science. The twin frames

play us out between them. We shift
restlessly around the blind spots, straining
to pinpoint exact echoes. I edge away,
aiming to see just you, see how much like you
this endless line of form can be. But I lose it
if I move too far. Or my feet are still in the picture.
It makes me want to get behind the mirror,
to peel down to the layer that's true. Caught
but not caught accurately enough, too many of me
crowd in, precise but separate. You move on. I watch
your repeated leaving, and stand for a moment.

Circus pony

Each evening after school you met
like lovers. You angled offerings
through the tired wire fence –
she accepted as the air accepts.
Among the traffic fumes and concrete,
her heavy eyes and warm saluting breath
became your fireside.

Every night you dreamed her
in the spotlight, all small girls
carried on her back, prettily
tramping the ring, high-kicking
over flames to gasps and applause
and for a finale leaping into darkness,
away from the crowds, the beatings.

And when you ran away at last,
north to the gleaming Fens,
you took a husband and a newborn
to be safe. Routines followed. Years
lost like old flames. Chosen
and not chosen became pathways.
Fences were your tightrope.

And when the circus came,
you took your daughter to the fence
to see the ponies waiting – wanting
her to sense that you had stood
daily by a tired wire fence,
calming the soft nose of a pony,
patient, headstrong, poised to bolt.

The florist

The florist tends her children like flowers
– shapes them with a knife,
murmurs love when no one listens,
digs their roots and upends them
when the spring takes her.

At night she listens to their sleeping
and dreams of forests
full of Wild Gladioli, Wood Sorrel,
Sundew, Cottongrass, Celandines
grappling towards sun.

In love's usefulness
her children nurture herbs,
learn to seize the small and pleasant
bitterness of thyme, shock of mint,
nestling breath of rosemary.

She helps them turn the soil,
spread the sand-like seeds,
scatter wishes for a sturdy crop.
Distant as a sunflower,
she turns towards them by degrees.

Old tricks

As if he can teach her to swim again
in that numbing pool on the Norfolk coast
with brother and sister dive-bombing
while he patiently pulls her forward, gripping hands.

First, both hers are gloved by his:
her body lifts as he tiptoes back,
taking her with him. Then his loosen,
retreat, coast around her unclosing fists.

A rare kiss of flesh becomes the only anchor
as his upturned palms glide beneath hers
– a first experience of flight, buoyed up,
surviving in two directions at once.

Finally, his presence drifts, leaving her
knuckles tensing, fists ready to close
and dive, testing her new weight
on the opening palm of the water.

Hopton-on-Sea

When I can clearly see the stars,
I aim, true as a laser beam, into space
and rebound, a child in your arms

shirking sleep, confident that I will be carried
from the Silver Dollar cabaret
to the cradle of the caravan.

The smell of the gas cooker warms us
more than its see-through blue. We sit on our beds
to eat. Prawn cocktail crisps and card games

punctuate the rain. The salt of sea and crackers
coats my lips like doughnut sugar. The sand
works my skin, smoothing, smoothing.

The chevronned, stainless steel steps,
removable, lead my jelly shoes to a world
of bare open skies.

The wind turbines

With angular grace,
they exercise their art in open fields.

I see the clean ploughs rise,
then crest and swoop.

Edged with light, they proffer
stillness, motion, purpose –

as they tumble the wind into live,
an army harvesting the air

bestowing the ghost of power
on the fathers, the sons.

Flow

An ancient Alaskan woman,
arthritic knees bent, dried-
up hands thrust in the waters,
pours her face towards me.

'What are you doing?'
My eyes form the question.
In reply, silence slips from her.
Blueness shines from her eyes.

Jutting from the top
of her apron pocket
is the mast of her mobile phone.
I see. She is pushing the river.

Darwin

Charles Darwin is white as spume,
his stomach a vortex.

His lips dry and cracked, holed up
in his cabin, he ventures only as far

as the rail to be sick.
He hasn't bargained on this,

could not prepare for the lurch
of the deck as the sea swells,

pushing his flimsy historical craft
about as it pleases.

*

She pauses, lays down the book
rushes to the bathroom

to be sick – the small swell
of her newly discovered bump

pushing her round as it pleases.
Lips dry and cracked, she picks the book

back up, keen to see how he fares.
Though she knows,

the part where he hasn't the guts
still hollows her out.

Picasso's cat

Cubists knew a good deal about quantum theory
– the oscillation between hard fact and art.

Schrödinger's famous cat in a box gets the point;
the astonishing state of possibilities.

After several hours of research,
Picasso chopped people up.

And then the box was opened –
one for the eye, one for the whiskers,

one for the tail. Let's go back.
We live in a moderately stable universe.

A cubist approach to an article by Ron Collins in *Nature*, vol. 443.

Moon child

The women are leaving the earth
by way of the moon
as it recedes each moment
inch by wary inch.

Meanwhile, the children continue
to be born towards the stars.

Their slight lives
exit the darkness at last,
pulled towards the receding light
that trammels their mothers.

As the moon-crab scuttles away,
drawing the tide back,

you sleep heavily
by my side in the moonlit night
while our three-year-old child
lies unmade in the bed between us.

Arachne

A spider in the morning, anguish.
A spider in the evening, hope.

FRENCH PROVERB

You tell me your dream
of the dead children.

Beneath my ribs spiders
stretch their outsized legs.

I feel them flex
and unfurl claws.

Their small bodies lift
and weigh forwards.

They are thin and awkward.
They are faster than I can think.

The spider's children wake
with her. Together they walk

into my bloodstream, rearing.

Smoke and apples

He holds fire, wasting in his hand.
The crumbling tip of ash

reaches for his tensed fist.
His fingers can't settle

on a grown-up hold.
Eye-level with the market stall –

a feast of apples, plums and tangerines –
he is entrusted with this strange creature.

He can only watch its fierce tip
slowly swallow the white.

He looks up at his mother
as she weighs each apple in her palm,

scrutinises each for the smallest flaw,
selects only those she wishes to consume.

The duty of balance I

Incendiary

During the Blitz, he said,
fire-raisers spat on his street.

Aircraft freed their bomblets at altitude,
blinding scraps of phosphorus

that consumed oxygen to flare,
grew as they fell, into scores of fires

– beacons for incoming bombers,
stowing their own DNA of damage.

Fierce white lumps scattered
like moon-rocks around.

As if in a trick, a man dropped a tin hat
on one on their doorstep.

The hat glowed white hot and altered.
He watched his mother watch.

Across the street, an unnatural brightness
challenged the blacked-out sky.

Through pink smoke he saw
barrage balloons guttering,

the odd genuine star,
smelled fumes like wild garlic.

On Victory Night the fireworks
went *boom, crump, crump* like guns.

Peace was declared in an excess of light
streaming strangely from windows.

He told me phosphorus means 'light bearer',
is built-in to all living cells.

'How many fell after the war?' he asked,
meaning his own story – meaning the way

he watched his mother's mind
for years after. Waited for it to ignite.

The duty of balance II

Oxygen

He was that age, fourteen,
his hormones already in trouble.
He stormed the stunted stairs of ruins,
challenged local gangs for turfs of rubble,
dodged the confines of the parlour
to haul what he could from childhood.

Though the war was four years back,
surprising things were rationed:
father's tolerance of questions,
the clarity of mother's mind.
Too much oxygen being lethal
as too little, he burnt what he could.

In a dream he saw the Northern Lights
pulse beneath the clouds of London,
lacking only the proper conditions
to show. Then streams of white ribbon
tore strips off the stars, tied the sky,
looped through their limits of colour.

When he woke his mother was dancing.
When he came home from school she was gone.

The duty of balance III

Northern Lights

Like she's just back from shopping
they said. He skulked in his room,
refused to acknowledge the door, her coat
as it sighed into place on the banister post.

He'd taken the *ill-advised* journey just once
to the low home with wheelchair-wide doors
filled with the drone and bark of inmates.
Tea in the dining hall was like flying –

everything altered, even her eyes.
Her pupils were gaping. The colours
of her iris shifted. For months
they'd tried to shock her back.

Now she was stowed in the house again,
he listened for silences. Father
fussed over lunch, requisitioned
his presence to bolster the troops.

She sat in her old chair politely.
He broke the code. Held her
like she was still gone. It felt
like that day in the bombed-out house

when the top stair crumbled – leaving
him flexed on the tip of things;
grasping the duty of balance,
gasping for something to give.

The four-minute war

The four-minute warning is over. It was a test.
The birds are gone. The grass grows towards the sun.
The snow is not ashes from the blast. It was a test.

For four minutes, my parents stood, shaking.
My father's hand jerked towards my mother's breast. She turned
away, towards the siren. My parents and I were shaken.

It was the war come back to claim them. Ice blood
stopped their veins. No thoughts. Simply the shrieking
sound and waiting for the blast: metal mashing into blood.

And then it stopped. The four minute warning was over.
I breathed again, forgot my fraction of their fear. It was
a test. For me, the four-minute warning stays over.

Commissioned for a London Science Museum Dana Centre
event on 'Emotional Contagion'.

Static

You collect it daily anywhere:
it amasses unnoticed

through contact with others,
objects, circumstances.

You're barely aware of the loss
as each charge transfers

from you, to you –
only noticing when

it sets itself down, connects
you again to the earth, like grief.

Commissioned for a London Science Museum Dana Centre
event on 'Electricity'.

Flight

The first indication of its presence:
the quality of your spit, flecked
with dark-brown spots and streaks;
the x-ray, strikingly banded black.

You took hollow hunting notes
of breath, clipping each intake.
Our conversations
were pointed and confused.

Frozen motionless by tubes,
hospital gave you
a bare patch on the throat
to breathe through, very small.

Rivals in persistence, you
and your rattling song
of astounding vehemence
cut black arcs across the sky.

Towards evening, you breathed
a prolonged stuttering scold,
familiar to everyone,
that terminates in flight.

White

Meanwhile, surely there must be something to say
W.S. GRAHAM, 'The Constructed Space'

Meanwhile, surely there must be something to say
about colour, and how it is only

the shades that an object rejects
that we see. Every thing

shows us the flip side of what we suppose.
And of course I think of white

when I say this – being almost all
colours thrown back.

Like the white sheets of your last bed,
with its tight hospital corners.

And your face, grown paler,
fending off more and more of the light.

Knell

At the bottom of the ocean it is not
quiet. From the middle of the maelstrom,
a ship releases its treasure.

Submerged, holed, its base black
with lichen, its rusted anchor coiled nearby,
its mast ripples in the blue on rising blue.

Flurries of rust float among shoals
of shining fish that only flash
from certain angles, in certain light.

The ship releases its elements,
adds itself to the sum
of carbon remaking a body.

Colours count themselves out and in.
The toughest metals crumble,
flake, turn small and soft.

All debris returns
to speckles of light,
lifts to the gentle surface

and breaks. All things
pixelate into atoms.
Nothing is lost. Nothing is lost.

Crossing the Arctic

He is coddled in ice, cold beyond knowing.
He recognises nothing, even himself.
Everywhere a strange quality of light.

Slowly his lips freeze shut. His eyebrows
bow to the weight of ice. Eyelashes
no longer flick to open.

Deep below ground, millennial ice
wordlessly rifts and breaks.
Rivers carve their artless future.

The Travelling Salesman Problem

Statistics are human beings with the tears wiped away.
PAUL BRODEUR

*Given a finite number of cities and the cost of travel between
each pair of them, find the cheapest way a salesman could visit
each city once and return to the starting point.*

He travels in the minds of mathematicians.
He has no form but going – a pure line
stretched across an unnamed land.

The assumption is he has no friends
or family to visit to divert his route.
There's no time for him to stop for food.

You will not see him
freewheel down the valley.
Or sit in jams that idly waste his fuel.

Seasons would affect
the price he has to pay
but where are they?

And what of all those things he's flogging:
jets and biros, tractors, axes, train-sets,
boxes, trucks...don't they slow him down?

Constant questions trail him. And for what?
All numbers are imaginary. But look,
here he comes towards us now,

wielding the calculator in *his* hand,
trying to fathom his value
and plot the point of his home.

Snakes

Your snakeskin gloves lie
furled on the hall table.

They've nested there
through spring and summer.

Now the cold is catching up,
your hands are elsewhere, exposed

or covered by unknown gloves,
unknown hands.

Your gloves are hibernating.
I haven't the power to wake them.

The hall is a cave I cross
avoiding their slow-pulsed stare.

Matryoshka I

The brides

Brides are the same in Russia
and different: that same expectation
of uniqueness – everything lifted

in a dress with ruches and bling,
flowers gripped pert in a waving hand,
ringleted hair that sets off a day-long crown,

the ring with the missing middle
finds its partner on the hand
of a boy her father never liked

and the mothers are drinking already,
standing apart, posing when asked
for pictures, carefully saying nothing.

Matryoshka II

Submariner

The submariner from Moldavia
forced to surface during Perestroika
when the State Bank sank
says he regrets everything
with a smile on his face.

The Nissan he once hocked for wood
to build this home hand over fist
rots in his good-life garden.
He says he feels blessed, missing
other lives: it multiplies you.

The gold cupolas of the town square
frame his middle shack. He plies us with
stories and vodka. Nothing goes to waste.
Even our guide with the potent blue eyes
sleeps well here, with no wish to surface.

Matryoshka III

Babushkas

This is a capital refashioning the past
literally. Everything comes with a backdrop
of scaffold and cranes and masking.
Whole blocks of the city are missing.
As marble slabs slot back into place,
Muscovites seem tuned to the sound.
Churches razed by Stalin, swapped
for bulky fifties blocks, come back to life
as Stalin's fancies are in turn erased.

In the middle, by the Moskva River,
the Assumption Cathedral rises again.
It gleams with gold-wrought gates
and icons, every inch freshly plastered
with frescoes. Cupolas are fringed
with workmen in jeans complaining
on mobiles. Orthodox priests text
their friends between masses. Babushkas
with covered hair move as if witnessing nothing.

Coleridge's second dream

At the wedding all dead sailors
take the ear of each guest.

All their boats are silent.
All their treasures gone.

Their mouths close only
on water; open to suck

on the rustle of wishes
each guest tides to the couple.

The holes of their eyes broken open,
they clack their bones at each jig.

They're here to blanch the marriage,
leach the booty in their turn.

The guests muse on them
stooped towards darkness.

But the couple, the couple
will sail tomorrow, and swim.

Schrödinger's pregnancy test

For her, theoretical physics
is a bird soaring next to a plane.

From her pressurised berth
she glimpses

movement, rising
out of reach.

All it takes
is a broad mauve line in a window

for it to land, bang
on her heart.

On seeing the furies in the sky

For all the world like a trio of wild-haired women
breasting out of that cloud – the prows of three ships
arms outstretched behind them, coasting the blue.

And why less real than this sunshine
back-lighting my garden, the halo
around the hedge, the green plastic chair

that holds my dreamlike limbs
– as unconnected to me as those three
on their way to vengeance against, please...

the summertime whine
of next door's boys, desperate to cry out,
and their hammering father.

One of them soon will raise
the first fist, the 'not fair' hymn
to the ignored mother I can hear

saying to no one listening,
no one at all but me, saying 'look,
look at those women up there, riding the day'.

Not the girl in this picture

She has no back, no shoulder, no arms.
Her legs are sliced off but she smiles.

Her boundaries are neatly defined.
She is leaning on herself

anchored already
in her own weight.

She has turned away from the water
towards the lens that lets me see her now.

She does not know
how the shutter works.

She has no need
to understand miracles.

The Art of Gentleness

When you burn a body
it reacts, even in death:

the knees jerk,
trying to sit

as the sinews shrivel,
contracting the surface.

The art
is to touch a flame

to living tissue, though it feels
dead, and remain still.

No such thing

Because meaning brims
almost always

and the air whistles
when it's cold.

Because my blood
is loud as light

and my bones tick
like growing wood.

Because I replay
birdsong in me

and nearly always word
my thoughts.

Because your echo
resounds through me

and I can hear
your misplaced voice.

Because somewhere, always,
there is not –

please don't tell me there
is silence.

Möbius strip

A simple science trick to try at home.
Half-twist a slip of paper. Link the ends
to make an 'O'. Take a pencil, trace a line that loops
the shape formed by the surface. See
how the in and out sides merge. The join
tangles dimensions. There's no front or back.

However many times you turn it on its back
it holds its simple seamless shape like home.
The connection goes beyond the fragile join:
it feeds itself with endless seeming ends
that work their way beyond what you can see
and turn your mind in questioning quick loops.

As your eye and mind work loops
trying to connect the front and back
you may brood over other things you see
or don't see. Like how 'now' always feels like home,
and yet so many moments all have ends
pulled tight through you without a join.

If you could ask your younger self to join
the many-voiced parade of you that loops
across the supple, unsubstantial ends
of days and hold your hand, and take you back
to then, and examine each clear particle of home
that was 'now' then, you'd see

some things the mind just isn't built to see.
There's no way to find the small, tight-focussed join
that makes this now, this here, so surely home
yet carries all the others in its loops
that time won't let you redo or take back,
but lets you trace the fragile, moving ends.

In photos, home-spun stories without ends
that parents tell a child, you can see
how hard you try to keep on turning back
to what and who and how you know – to join
this 'now', through blind, reflexive loops,
to something else and make yourself a home.

Make a mass of loops at home and see
how the joins make countless starts and ends.
And think of 'now' as home. You can't go back.

Shoe, 1979

I have this image of me
that's almost the picture:
gap grin, hedge hair, stripy-tee,
with long childish bones,
on a log bench raised in a river,
West Acre, the 1970s.
My legs are dangling in the flow,
arms angled, clinging on,

I'm surrounded by relatives.
And some time before or after
the shutter snapped,
my white jelly shoe slipped
into the murk below.
I couldn't retrieve it.
Even if somehow it was there now,
it must have grown out of me.

Flickr

How quickly each country contracts
to thirty-six bits. Civilisation shrinks
to extras, props, perspective.
People edge out of the shot and the sky
remains grey over some Square, forever.

Behind the fading domes of the soon
misplaced monastery, the stars
ape souvenirs. Each bauble melts
into another country's keepsake
within weeks. The fact of being

far away recedes, becomes a fiction
you tell yourself over and over.
You check the evidence often,
lacking something to hold
in your hand and believe. Like this.

Aurora

I am waiting for aberrations of light.

For quiet curves to arc and flutter,
to break into form.

For the skiffle of static to announce
shifting centres
of green, violet, white-blue –
colour as its own pure note,
a Kandinsky composition.

For contours to shape the charged air –
now a back-lit mountain, now a man
emerging from his own electric shadow.

For guttering light to veil the moon
and stars, unveil them.

While every poem ever written
about the moon rises before me,
I wait here, in the dark,

with my eyes wide open.